GOING HOME
An Epic Saga in Sixteen Snippets

by the same author

Aunt Mildred's Parrot

Some Skulduggery at the Banana Warehouse

and also available from Paperweight Press

GOING HOME
An Epic Saga in Sixteen Snippets

Ian Harding

**Paperweight
Press**

Copyright Notice

First published in the UK in 2002 by Paperweight Press

Paperweight Press, Springfield House,
5 Spring Hill Terrace, Whitby, North Yorkshire, YO21 1EG

Going Home
Copyright © 1997 Ian Harding

All rights reserved. No part of this manuscript may be reproduced, stored in a retrieval system, or transmitted, in any form or by any means, electronic, mechanical, photocopying, recording or otherwise, without the prior written permission of the copyright owner.

No performance of this play may be given without a licence which must be obtained from the publisher before rehearsals commence.

Ian Harding is hereby identified as author of this work in accordance with section 77 of the Copyright, Designs and Patents Act 1988.

This publication is sold subject to the condition that it shall not, by way of trade or otherwise, be lent, resold, hired out or otherwise circulated without the publisher's prior consent in any form of binding or cover other than that in which it is published and without a similar condition being imposed on the subsequent purchaser.

ISBN 1-903477-06-9 Bound

ISBN 1-903477-07-7 Unbound

Typeset in 10 on 12 pt Griffo Schoolbook

Printed and bound by Paperweight Press

Cast, in order of appearance

DR KERENHAPPUCH, an academic
Four BELIEVERS
A MINISTER of religion
HANNAH, a woman, later mother of SARAH
JOACHIM, a man, later father of SARAH
PROFESSOR ABDIEL, a surgeon
DR ELEAZAR, a surgeon
A NURSE
MR HEZEKIAH, a surgeon
SARAH, a girl, aged ten, later fourteen, later eighteen
MISS HEPHZIBAH, a schoolteacher
GABRIELLE, a girl, friend of SARAH
JEMIMA, a girl, friend of SARAH
MIRIAM, a girl, friend of SARAH
The voice of LORD AIDAN, a Supreme Being

Going Home was first performed in Maseru, Kingdom of Lesotho at the Machabeng Theatre on the 29th May 1997.

GOING HOME

First Snippet	The Prologue
Second Snippet	The Ceremony
Third Snippet	The Baby
Fourth Snippet	The Implant
Fifth Snippet	The Question
Sixth Snippet	The Lesson
Seventh Snippet	The Legend
Eighth Snippet	The Doubt
Ninth Snippet	The Party
Tenth Snippet	The Discovery
Eleventh Snippet	The Linking
Twelfth Snippet	The Vision
Thirteenth Snippet	The Speech
Fourteenth Snippet	The Guilt
Fifteenth Snippet	The Reality of Paradise
Sixteenth Snippet	The Epilogue

First Snippet – Prologue

The houselights are still on. DR KERENHAPPUCH *enters via the* CENTRE *entrance. Applause.*

DR KEREN   Good Afternoon Ladies and Gentlemen, and welcome to the first of my lectures on Greek Myths and Legends, which concerns the story of Prometheus and Vulturius.

According to Greek Mythology, at the time of Creation, man was the weakest of all creatures, naked, cold and miserable.

The Demigod Prometheus took pity on the poor creature, and gave him fire to enable him to conquer the night, frighten away animals, work metals and gradually develop technology.

However, Prometheus did this at great risk, because he stole the fire from the Sun.

When Zeus, the King of the Gods, found out about this, he was very angry indeed.

Zeus ordered that Prometheus was to be taken to the very end of the World, and there chained to a rock.

Every day, a vulture was sent by Zeus, to bite and tear at Prometheus' liver, but at night the vulture went away, and miraculously his liver grew back again, so that he would be ready for more torture on the next day. This, then, is the story of Prometheus. A sort of Ancient Greek version of the Robin Hood legend. Prometheus, who stole from the rich to give to poor mankind. Thank you for your attention, Ladies and Gentlemen. My next lecture will be at the same time next week.

Applause. DR KERENHAPPUCH *leaves RIGHT. A pause of approximately 15 seconds to allow the audience time to become puzzled and restless. Blackout.*

Second Snippet – The Ceremony

Music 1 during which the stage is set to represent a church. From blackout a BELIEVER *enters under blue light through the RIGHT entrance, carrying a candle. She lights the Floor Candle which is near the CENTRE entrance, which has been brought on under the blackout by the* MINISTER. *Lights up slightly. She exits LEFT. Four* BELIEVERS *bring four benches, two through the LEFT entrance and two through the RIGHT entrance, placing them so as to represent the pews in a church. They seat themselves on the benches. A gobo in the shape of a cross is projected onto the floor, head toward the CENTRE entrance. The* MINISTER *enters CENTRE carrying the Book of Instructions and takes up a position at the head of the cross. A Man (*JOACHIM*) enters through the LEFT entrance and simultaneously a Woman (*HANNAH*) enters through the RIGHT entrance. They take up positions in front of the* MINISTER *and kneel. A shaft of bright light, representing the Supreme Being, appears in front of the* MINISTER. *As the music closes, lights on the* MINISTER, HANNAH *and* JOACHIM *up considerably.*

MINISTER   Dearly Beloved, we are gathered here today to witness the joining of this man and this woman in the state of honourable and proper pair bonding. They have been carefully chosen for compatibility by our Guardian, the Lord Aidan, who, in His infinite wisdom knows and understands the complete genetic characteristics of every one of us. The bonding of these two young people will result in the joyful creation of a New Child, which will restore our island's population to the three thousand allowed us according to the Book of Instructions which has been handed down to us by our mothers and

4   GOING HOME

                fathers and their mothers and fathers before them. Come, my people, we must rejoice in the death of our brother Matthew at the age of one hundred and seventeen, which has created the imbalance in our numbers and permitted todays' happy event to take place.

BELIEVERS   We give honour to the memory of Matthew who has let go of life in order that a New Child may be granted us, and to the Lord Aidan for choosing the child's parents with such wisdom.

MINISTER   Arise, my children.

HANNAH and JOACHIM stand before the MINISTER.

MINISTER   By the power vested in me by the Book of Instructions, and under the guidance of our Guardian, the Lord Aidan, without whose benevolence and wisdom we should surely be unable to maintain our population so precisely, I name you, Hannah, to be the mother of the New Child. Do you, Hannah, understand the significance of this event?

HANNAH   I do.

MINISTER   By the power vested in me by the Book of Instructions, and under the guidance of our Guardian, the Lord Aidan, without whose benevolence and wisdom we should surely be unable to maintain our population so precisely, I name you, Joachim, to be the father of the New Child. Do you, Joachim, understand the significance of this event?

JOACHIM   I do.

THE CEREMONY 5

MINISTER	I am authorized to tell you that, due to the combinations of your genetic characteristics which have been carefully selected by the Lord Aidan for his wondrous purposes which are so far beyond our understanding, it is hereby decreed that you will create a girl-child and that she will be called Sarah.
BELIEVERS	We give honour to Hannah and Joachim, the parents elect of the New Girl-Child Sarah, who will conform exactly to the genetic requirements of the Lord Aidan, whose benevolence we cherish and whose powers and purposes are beyond our understanding.
H. and J.	We give honour to the Lord Aidan for granting us the privilege of creating the New Sarah, who will fulfil His wondrous and unknown purposes just as we have done, and our parents before us, and their parents before them.
MINISTER	You may now hold hands.

HANNAH *and* JOACHIM *do so*.

MINISTER	The Bond is placed. I now pronounce you the Parents Elect of the New Sarah.
BELIEVERS	Honoured are the Parents Elect of the New Sarah.

HANNAH *and* JOACHIM *remain spotlit as Music 2 begins and the stage is cleared.*

Third Snippet – The Baby

Music 2 during which the stage is cleared and reset under blue light. The benches are removed by the BELIEVERS, *two via the* LEFT *entrance and two via the* RIGHT *entrance. The* MINISTER *leaves by the* CENTRE *entrance with the Book of Instructions and the floor candle. An Armchair and a Sofa, on which is a blanket, are brought on through the* LEFT *and* RIGHT *entrances by the* BELIEVERS *who then exit via the* LEFT *and* RIGHT *entrances. As the music closes,* HANNAH *and* JOACHIM *turn to face each other.*

HANNAH   Come on Joachim, put your hand here. Feel the baby.

JOACHIM   I'm not sure I should. Suppose I hurt her.

HANNAH   Don't be so silly. How can you hurt her while she's still safe inside me? Come on!

HANNAH takes JOACHIM's hand and places it firmly upon her abdomen, holding it there.

HANNAH   There! Can you feel her? Feel her kicking. Ow!

JOACHIM   Yes, I can feel her. Isn't it bad for you?

JOACHIM takes his hand away.

HANNAH   Bad for me? Of course it isn't. It's just a bit uncomfortable, sometimes.

JOACHIM   I think you should rest, Hannah. I really do. Why don't you sit down?

JOACHIM leads HANNAH to the sofa and makes her comfortable. He sits in the armchair.

HANNAH	Yes, thank you Joachim, that does feel better. It can get quite tiring carrying this weight about in front of me…

A pause

HANNAH	Joachim…
JOACHIM	Yes?
HANNAH	Joachim, just think. As soon as Sarah is born, our population will be back to exactly three thousand, and it's all happening through us. Isn't it exciting?
JOACHIM	It's an honour. The Lord Aidan has created a New Child, and He has chosen us to help him in his task. We will not fail him.
HANNAH	Of course we won't…

A pause

HANNAH	Joachim…
JOACHIM	What is it Hannah? Are you worried that something will go wrong? That there is something wrong with Sarah? Tell me, Hannah!
HANNAH	No, it's not that. I'm sure there's nothing wrong with her. There's certainly nothing wrong with her legs, anyway. Ow!
JOACHIM	Then what is it? There's something bothering you, I can tell.
HANNAH	Come closer, Joachim. Put your head near her.

JOACHIM *kneels next to* HANNAH. *She holds his head and places it on her abdomen. This is rather difficult and uncomfortable for* JOACHIM.

JOACHIM	Hannah! What is this all about?
HANNAH	Shhh! Keep quiet and still, and let your mind go blank.

JOACHIM	What? I don't understand.
HANNAH	Shhh!

A pause.

JOACHIM	What is this, Hannah? Am I supposed to hear something?
HANNAH	Can't you?
JOACHIM	No. If I knew what I was listening for, it might be easier.

He moves his head away from her, and kneels beside her. HANNAH *is rather annoyed.*

HANNAH	Oh! You're so insensitive. Why on Earth did the Lord Aidan choose you as Sarah's father. There must be plenty of other men who could have done a better job!

JOACHIM *is also becoming angry. He sits in the armchair.*

JOACHIM	Hannah! How dare you question the wisdom of the Lord Aidan. How can you presume to know better than he? That is blasphemy! We were chosen because of our genetic characteristics, as you know perfectly well. Only in that way will the child be perfect. Think what sort of children people would have if they were allowed to choose for themselves who to pair-bond with. The idea is ridiculous. I'm surprised at you for even thinking about it!

HANNAH *calms down a little, and starts to cry a little.*

HANNAH	Oh Joachim! I'm sorry. I didn't mean to question the Lord Aidan. I think I'm just getting worried about the responsibility of carrying the New Child. Why did He choose me, Joachim? Why me?

JOACHIM *calms down.*

JOACHIM   Because you are the best person for the job, Hannah. And you're questioning Him again. I think you must be very tired, and you can't think sensibly. Stop worrying about it.

HANNAH   You're right. Perhaps I should try to sleep.

She stretches out on the sofa. JOACHIM *wraps the blanket round her. A pause.*

HANNAH   Joachim…

JOACHIM   Go to sleep.

HANNAH   Joachim, are you sure you couldn't hear anything? It's just that – I can. I can hear her – in my mind, I think. It's as if she's trying to talk to me, but I can't understand what she's saying. Joachim, what do you think it means?

JOACHIM   Well, it means – it means… I don't know what it means! Do you mean that she's trying to communicate with you, before she's even born?

HANNAH   Yes – I think so.

JOACHIM   How?

HANNAH   I don't really know. Telepathy? I don't understand it, but you know you thought I was worried that there was something wrong with her? There isn't. I know there isn't anything wrong with her, she's fine. But I don't know how I know, if you see what I mean. I – I think she told me.

JOACHIM   What do you mean, told you?

THE BABY 11

HANNAH   What I'm saying. It's as if she can speak to me already. But not with her voice, and not with words. But I know she's all right, and she's happy. Joachim, do you think the Lord Aidan knew this when he chose us to be Sarah's parents? Did he know she would be like this? She is special, Joachim. Very special.

JOACHIM   We should not trouble ourselves with speculation as to what the Lord Aidan has planned. We cannot understand His powers and his wisdom. If he has created this child to be special in some way, that is his affair, not ours, but I think, probably, knowing how tired you are, that you are probably imagining it.

HANNAH *gets agitated again.*

HANNAH   Imagining it! Imagining it? I am not! Sarah is special and it is the Lord Aidan's will that she be so. Furthermore, I'll tell you something else. I've been searching through the database for details of all children born on this island for as far back as the records go, which is about eight hundred years, as far as I can gather. Never before has there been any instance of a child communicating with its mother before it was born, never!

JOACHIM   Records can be changed.

HANNAH   What would be the point? People would find out after it was born. If it were telepathy, I mean. No, Sarah is the first, and the Lord Aidan has arranged for it to be so. He must have been planning this for centuries! Yes, it's all making sense now. We don't choose who are to be parents, the Lord Aidan does. He knows all our

	genetic characteristics. We've been selectively bred, Joachim; carefully chosen so that eventually two parents will produce a special child. And we are those two parents! I know, Joachim, I know!
JOACHIM	Why would he go to all that trouble? Centuries of work, just so that you can tell that Sarah is all right. There have been healthy babies before, without any need for all that.
HANNAH	Joachim! You're missing the point! And now you're questioning the Lord Aidan too. Who are we to ask why? But it's true, Joachim, I can tell. And it must mean…
JOACHIM	What? What must it mean?
HANNAH	If the Lord Aidan has arranged for a child like this to be born – a child with special powers that nobody else has – there must be a reason. We don't know what the reason is – probably our intelligence is too limited to understand the reason even if we did know – but that doesn't prevent the reason from existing. The Lord Aidan knows the reason – and – must have known the reason for hundreds of years! Joachim – I'm frightened!
JOACHIM	Because, if you're right, the reason is about to happen?
HANNAH	It must be, mustn't it? If the reason wasn't about to happen, He wouldn't have arranged for Sarah to be born now.
JOACHIM	I think we have a little longer.
HANNAH	What do you mean?

JOACHIM	If Sarah is as special as you believe, and I'm starting to think you may be right…
HANNAH	I am right!
JOACHIM	Then I suspect she will be able to understand the reason too.
HANNAH	But how can she? She isn't even born yet.
JOACHIM	That's exactly what I mean. If the Lord Aidan has some reason for creating a child with special powers, He will need those powers to mature before they can be used properly. He will want her to grow up before her powers are needed, and we are the ones who have been chosen to look after her while she does.
HANNAH	Oh, I see. Yes, you're right, you must be right. He will have planned her birth to be enough in advance of – whatever the reason is – so that she will be grown up before He needs her.
JOACHIM	Of course. The Lord Aidan is always kind and looks after the people well. He will wait until she is grown, so stop worrying. Come on, I think it is time you actually went to bed. You won't sleep properly lying on that sofa.

JOACHIM *helps* HANNAH *to get up, and steadies her as they begin to exit RIGHT. As they go…*

HANNAH	But Joachim, won't she be in danger? If the reason is so important that the Lord Aidan needs to create a special child to help him, then won't it be dangerous? Can't we warn her? Can we look after her while she grows up, and not tell her? Will He let us tell her?

JOACHIM	Hannah, if she's as special as you say – if she can tell you that she's happy – she knows, Hannah, she knows.

They exit. Lights fade to black. Sound of baby crying.

HANNAH	{*off*} But why, Joachim? Why have they taken our baby away from us?
JOACHIM	{*off*} The Lord Aidan's baby, Hannah. Anyway, you heard the doctor. Once she's had the operation she can come back to us, and live with us until she's grown up.
HANNAH	{*off*} But she's not happy, Joachim. I know.
JOACHIM	{*off*} Tell her you love her.

Fourth Snippet – The Implant

Music 3. Under blue light, the armchair and sofa are struck via the LEFT and RIGHT entrances. An operating theatre table is brought on via the CENTRE entrance by three surgeons and a nurse who crowd around the table, preventing the audience from seeing the baby.

PROF ABDIEL Friends and colleagues. This is an historic occasion. We are commanded by the Lord Aidan to insert into the brain of this baby girl, the New Sarah, a microchip, which my colleague Dr. Eleazar will now show to you.

Dr. Eleazar holds up the microchip, in a protective case.

DR ELEAZAR Ladies and Gentlemen. This is the microchip referred to by my colleague, Professor Abdiel. It has been designed and constructed by the Lord Aidan himself. Its purpose, however, is unknown to us.

PROF ABDIEL Never before have we been called upon to perform brain surgery on so young a patient. Naturally, we are apprehensive. If something should go wrong… No. Let us give honour to the Lord Aidan that he may be with us, and guide us, in this most delicate of tasks.

ALL *{to each other}* May the Lord Aidan be with you.

PROF ABDIEL We will now begin the operation. Mr. Hezekiah will make the preliminary incision by drilling into the skull and removing a small piece of it.

NURSE	Excuse me, Mr. Hezekiah. Is there a special part of the skull that you must drill through?
MR HEZEKIAH	Oh yes, naturally. The microchip has to be carefully positioned in the baby's brain so that it can be connected directly to the language centre.
NURSE	Why is that, Mr. Hezekiah?
MR HEZEKIAH	To be quite honest, nurse, I do not know myself. Professor Abdiel has received instructions from the Lord Aidan concerning this. Is that not so, Professor?
PROF ABDIEL	That is correct, yes. First it was necessary to perform a CT scan of the child's head. The data from this was given to the Lord Aidan, who then advised me of the exact coordinates for the location of the microchip. I have also instructions explaining precisely how the chip is to be connected to the brain. This part of the operation is the responsibility of Dr. Eleazar.
NURSE	How will the connection be carried out, Doctor?
DR ELEAZAR	It is a relatively straightforward task, although accuracy is of the utmost importance. Electrodes are connected to the chip, and the ends of these electrodes are inserted directly into the brain tissue. Since the brain operates by means of electrical signals, these signals can be conveyed to the chip.
NURSE	And why is it important for the child's brain to communicate with the chip?
DR ELEAZAR	On that subject I cannot help you, I'm afraid, because, of course, we know nothing about the Lord Aidan's purpose in this respect.

THE IMPLANT 17

HANNAH	{*off, screaming*} Joachim!
JOACHIM	{*off, agitated*} What is it, Hannah? Whatever is the matter?
HANNAH	{*off, in tears*} I can't feel her, Joachim. She's not there.
JOACHIM	{*off*} What do you mean, she's not there? Not where? Not in the operating theatre?
HANNAH	{*off*} Yes. No. I mean, I don't know. She was unhappy, remember? I can tell whether she's happy, even when she's not with me…
JOACHIM	{*off*} Yes, telepathy or something, right?
HANNAH	{*off*} Right. And then I told her – thought to her – that I loved her, just as you said, and she started to calm down.
JOACHIM	{*off*} Good.
HANNAH	{*off, in tears*} But, but now I can't tell whether she's happy or not. I can't get anything from her at all! Oh, Joachim – I think she's – dead!
JOACHIM	{*off*} No, Hannah. She can't be. The doctors would have told us…
HANNAH	{*off*} Then why can't I feel her…?
JOACHIM	{*off*} …she's unconscious. Yes, that's it. The doctors will have anaesthetized her for the operation.

HANNAH	{*off, in tears*} But they don't, Joachim. Not for brain surgery. They keep the patient conscious so that they can tell if anything goes wrong. There are no nerves in the brain, you see, so it doesn't hurt and – and – something has gone wrong, hasn't it, Joachim. {*losing control*} Why did the Lord Aidan make her have this operation? She's only a baby, and now my baby's – dead!

A pause, during which HANNAH *cries uncontrollably.*

PROF ABDIEL	Astonishing!
NURSE	Professor Abdiel?
PROF ABDIEL	Never have I seen a patient react to such traumatic surgery as this one. There must be something very unusual about her.
DR ELEAZAR	{*anxiously*} What is wrong? I am just inserting the electrodes. Is there a problem with the patient, Professor?
MR HEZEKIAH	{*relieved*} There is no problem, Doctor. Our patient is simply fast asleep. And looking at the electroencephalograph readings, a very deep sleep at that.
NURSE	How can she possibly fall asleep during an operation? Do you mean natural sleep?
PROF ABDIEL	This is most unusual. I find it very hard to believe that a baby could fall asleep under these conditions, with bright lights and the four of us talking all around her. It's as if... No...
NURSE	Professor?
PROF ABDIEL	If I didn't know it was impossible, I would say that she has done this herself. Made herself go to sleep.

THE IMPLANT 19

MR HEZEKIAH	Quite impossible.
PROF ABDIEL	Oh, I've known people who could do it – make themselves go to sleep at will – anywhere, any time. But I'm talking about adults, not a baby only a few days old. And yet…
DR ELEAZAR	Well, whatever the cause, it means we can't find out whether the operation has been successful until she wakes up.
HANNAH	{*off, hysterical*} Sarah's dead! They've killed my baby! The Lord Aidan has killed my baby!
JOACHIM	{*off*} Hannah…
PROF ABDIEL	Have you completed the connections, Doctor?
DR ELEAZAR	I have. It only remains for Mr. Hezekiah to close up the skull, and then she can be transferred to intensive care to recover from the trauma.
PROF ABDIEL	Before Mr. Hezekiah does so, we must wake her to make sure that her brain functions are normal. There are no unusual signs from the electro-encephalograph but I am not prepared to take any unnecessary risks. Wake her, nurse… …By the Lord Aidan…
HANNAH	{*off*} Joachim!
NURSE	Professor! She's waking! All by herself. It's exactly as if she knew…
MR HEZEKIAH	And the readings – look at the readings!
JOACHIM	{*off*} Hannah?
PROF ABDIEL	This is quite amazing.
DR ELEAZAR	She's responding as if the operation had never taken place. The microchip is a part of her, now, and for ever, as if it had always been so.

NURSE	Honour to the Lord Aidan for our success in the operation.
ALL	Honour to the Lord Aidan.
NURSE	Look! She's smiling! How can a baby of that age smile!
PROF ABDIEL	This is a most unusual child, nurse. A most unusual child. The Lord Aidan has created her through Hannah and Joachim, and the Lord Aidan has guided us through this operation. She is the Lord Aidan's child, created for His wondrous purposes, too mysterious for us to comprehend. She is special, nurse. Take care of her now. I must go and tell the good news to Hannah and Joachim. They must be very worried about their daughter.
HANNAH	{*off, excited*} Joachim! She's alive!
JOACHIM	{*off, excited*} Alive! Hannah! Can you feel her again?
HANNAH	{*off, excited*} Yes! She's been asleep! She told me she was asleep. She – she told me – she told me it would be easier that way, for her – Joachim – how can she know all this? She knows about the microchip. How can she know about the microchip, Joachim? She's only a baby!
JOACHIM	{*off*} A special baby, Hannah. A very special baby.
HANNAH	{*off*} She's coming home, Joachim. Soon.
PROF ABDIEL	Thanks be to the Lord Aidan.
ALL	Thanks be to the Lord Aidan.

Blackout. The surgeons and nurse strike the operating table via the CENTRE entrance.

Fifth Snippet – The Question

HANNAH, JOACHIM and SARAH, aged 10, enter RIGHT. HANNAH carries a picnic basket, SARAH a bucket and spade. JOACHIM has a newspaper and a deckchair which he proceeds to erect. He sits, and has his back to the others throughout.

HANNAH	This is a nice spot, don't you think, Joachim?
JOACHIM	It'll do. At least I can sit and read the paper while Sarah plays on the sand.
SARAH	{*sitting CENTRE*} I'm going to make a sand castle, Daddy. Do you want to help?
JOACHIM	Later, perhaps.
HANNAH	{*sitting CENTRE*} You ought to give the child more attention, Joachim. How is she going to learn if you don't talk to her?

During the next, SARAH starts to build a sand castle.

JOACHIM	Can't I be allowed to read the newspaper in peace? I'll help her with the sand castle later.
HANNAH	Promise?
JOACHIM	Yes, promise. Now let me read the paper!
SARAH	This is the best beach on the whole island, Mummy. It's sheltered from the wind by that headland.

During the next, HANNAH puts a tablecloth on the sand and unpacks the basket.

HANNAH	That's what makes it so good for a picnic. Are you hungry?

SARAH	Mmmm. And thirsty. The sun's very hot today. How long before it goes out?
HANNAH	We've got about another four hours. Here, have some lemonade.
SARAH	Thanks, Mummy.
HANNAH	Joachim, do you want anything to drink?
JOACHIM	A cup of tea would be nice. It says here {*indicating newspaper*} that some fishermen cut through the shark nets and went outside.
HANNAH	Never!
JOACHIM	Apparently. Happened the night before last.
HANNAH	Did they get attacked?
JOACHIM	No. They got away with it, luckily for them.
HANNAH	The fools! They could have all been eaten alive. Think what that would do to the population control. Does the Lord Aidan know?
JOACHIM	Of course! Don't be stupid, Hannah.
HANNAH	What happened?
JOACHIM	Oh, they were summoned, of course. They had to repair the nets. Luckily for the rest of us, no sharks got in while they were broken.
SARAH	Daddy, what's a shark?
JOACHIM	Well, it's a bit like a big fish, but it isn't a fish. It lives in the sea and it has huge teeth and eats anything it can get hold of.
SARAH	Have you ever seen one?
JOACHIM	No, not personally. I don't want to either. I don't want to be eaten.
SARAH	Have you seen one, Mummy?

THE QUESTION 23

HANNAH	No, dear. That's why we have the nets. If we didn't have the nets the sharks could come in close to the beaches and it wouldn't be safe to go swimming.
SARAH	If you haven't seen one, how do you know that they exist?
HANNAH	What a silly question, Sarah! What would be the point of having the nets if they didn't exist? Anyway, if you want to see one, just look them up on the computer. After that, you won't want to see one for real, I can tell you!
SARAH	I don't think they exist. I think they're just made up to frighten people.
JOACHIM	Sarah! What are you talking about?
SARAH	I think the Lord Aidan made them up to frighten people, and He put the nets round the island to make the story more convincing. I don't think there are such things as sharks at all!
JOACHIM	Sarah! That is blasphemy, child! I'll wash your mouth out with soap when we get home!
HANNAH	But Sarah, how can there be pictures of them if they aren't real?
SARAH	Pictures can be faked, Mummy. You haven't seen one, Daddy hasn't either. Do you know anyone who has seen one?
HANNAH	Well…
SARAH	Daddy?
JOACHIM	Not as such, no…
SARAH	Well then. Mummy, may I have one of those sandwiches, please?
HANNAH	Oh! Yes, of course, dear.

SARAH	And some cake?
HANNAH	Mmmm… {*aside to* JOACHIM} Joachim, what's the matter with her? Can she be right? Is it all a story? You said the fishermen got back safely – perhaps there are no sharks after all… But why would the Lord Aidan pretend there are?
JOACHIM	Hannah, remember when she was tiny, you said she was special? Perhaps she is right, but I'm not going outside the nets to find out. Anyway, if the Lord Aidan has a reason, I'm sure it will be a good one. {*A thought*} Can't you use telepathy to talk to her about it – find out what she's thinking?
HANNAH	Oh, that doesn't work any more. Well, I think it would work, if she let it, but she doesn't. She keeps what she's thinking to herself these days. Still, she is the Lord Aidan's child, so I suppose we mustn't criticize. She does have some strange ideas, though.
SARAH	Mummy, how big is the island?
HANNAH	Oh, about 30 square kilometres, I think.

During the next, SARAH *folds a piece of paper to make an aeroplane.*

SARAH	And everyone that is, lives on the island?
HANNAH	Yes, of course.
SARAH	What's outside, beyond the nets?
HANNAH	Nothing really. Just the sea. Nobody ever goes there.
SARAH	Because of the sharks?
HANNAH	Yes.
SARAH	Which don't exist.

THE QUESTION 25

HANNAH	Which don't… You don't know that, Sarah.
SARAH	I do. Can I have some peanuts?
HANNAH	{*troubled*} What? Oh, peanuts. Yes.

SARAH *throws her paper aeroplane out to sea.*

SARAH	Look what I've made!
HANNAH	{*shocked*} Sarah! What do you think you're doing?
JOACHIM	{*angrily*} Sarah! Did you throw that?
SARAH	Yes, Daddy.
JOACHIM	Don't let me ever catch you doing that again! Don't you know the laws? The Lord Aidan will not permit flying machines in any shape or form!
SARAH	But it was only a…
JOACHIM	Be quiet, child! Not another word about it! {*to* HANNAH} I'm surprised you didn't notice what she was doing and stop her before it was too late. The Lord Aidan will find out, of course, and then we will be in trouble.
HANNAH	I'm sorry, Joachim. I was so busy thinking about the sharks…
JOACHIM	That is enough! I came here for some quiet relaxation and all we do is have an argument. I'm going to sleep.
SARAH	Aren't you going to help me with my sand castle, Daddy?
JOACHIM	Not after that, No!
HANNAH	I'll help you, Sarah. But you must promise not to make any more paper aeroplanes.

SARAH	All right, Mummy, but I don't understand why they're not allowed.
HANNAH	It's the law, Sarah. The Lord Aidan's law.
SARAH	But why? Doesn't He want people to have flying machines?
HANNAH	I suppose not. I've never really thought about it before.
SARAH	Well, I'm thinking about it, and it makes sense! It's the same reason that everyone believes in sharks! He doesn't want us to go outside — to find out what's outside!
HANNAH	But why not, Sarah?
SARAH	I don't know. Not yet. But I'm going to find out!
HANNAH	Oh, Sarah! You mustn't! If the Lord Aidan doesn't want us to go outside, then it must be dangerous. Please don't try to go through the net.
SARAH	Don't worry, Mummy. I'm not going to find out that way! I'll ask my teacher at school. She'll know why!

Lights fade to black. HANNAH, JOACHIM *and* SARAH *exit via the* CENTRE *entrance. Music 5 during which the set is changed to the classroom under blue light.*

Sixth Snippet – The Lesson

Music 5. Exeunt HANNAH, JOACHIM *and* SARAH, *under the blackout. The blue lights come up and four school desks and chairs are brought on by four students, one of whom is* SARAH, *from the CENTRE entrance. The students sit. As the music closes and the lights change,* MISS HEPHZIBAH *enters via the CENTRE entrance. The students stand.*

MISS HEPHZIBAH Good Morning, children.

STUDENTS Good Morning, Miss Hephzibah.

MISS HEPHZIBAH You may sit.

The students sit.

MISS HEPHZIBAH Well now, today is the last day of our school term, so I am going to let you choose what we do. Put up your hand if you have an idea.

All the students raise their hands.

MISS HEPHZIBAH Gabrielle, what would you like to do?

GABRIELLE Please, Miss Hephzibah, I'd like to go home.

The other students start to laugh.

MISS HEPHZIBAH Class! Stop that at once! Really, Gabrielle, I'm surprised at you. Now, has anyone got any sensible suggestions?

The other three raise their hands again.

JEMIMA Miss! Miss!

MISS HEPHZIBAH Don't call out, Jemima. Now you can wait your turn. What do you think we should do, Miriam?

MIRIAM I was wondering if I might be allowed to read my book, Miss. It's a very exciting story.

MISS HEPHZIBAH Well, that would depend on whether the others have books to read as well. {*To the others*} Do you?

The other students shake their heads.

JEMIMA Miss! Miss!

MISS HEPHZIBAH Jemima! How many more times do I have to tell you? Very well, what is it?

JEMIMA Perhaps you could read Miriam's book out loud to us. I'd like you to tell us a story.

MISS HEPHZIBAH Perhaps, but we ought to hear what Sarah suggests first. Sarah?

SARAH I would like to hear you tell us a story, Miss Hephzibah, but I would rather it were a true story.

MISS HEPHZIBAH A true story? What do you mean, Sarah?

SARAH Well, Mummy and Daddy and I were having a picnic on the beach, and I started thinking about the island, and how everybody lives on it, and nowhere else, and I started wondering about why, and what's out there, across the sea. And I thought you might know.

MISS HEPHZIBAH Did you now? Well, I do know, as it happens, but... Oh, I suppose you're all big enough by now to understand it. Yes, I'll tell you the story.

All four together:

GABRIELLE Not History, please!

MIRIAM I want to read my book!

JEMIMA Sarah! Why did you ask that?

SARAH Goody!

THE LESSON

MISS HEPHZIBAH Right, children. Make yourselves comfortable, and I'll begin. Once upon a time, people lived all over the Earth. There was lots of land, and it was divided up into different parts called countries, and the people were different too.

JEMIMA People are different now, Miss.

MISS HEPHZIBAH Yes, I know, Jemima. But in those days, different people lived in different parts of the world, and didn't talk to each other much.

MIRIAM I know about that, Miss. They all spoke different languages.

GABRIELLE Yes, and they believed in different Gods! I read that somewhere.

MISS HEPHZIBAH That's right Gabrielle. They didn't all believe in the Lord Aidan, as we do. In fact, I have a feeling that they never even saw their Gods. How strange.

GABRIELLE Do you mean, that when they went to church to talk to their Gods, the Gods didn't appear and speak to them, like the Lord Aidan does?

MISS HEPHZIBAH Yes. I know it's difficult to believe, but that's how it used to be.

SARAH But what happened to them, Miss Hephzibah? Did they all die or something?

MIRIAM Perhaps the Lord Aidan punished them for not believing in Him.

MISS HEPHZIBAH There are some people who think that is exactly what happened, Miriam. They believe He caused a great plague which spread throughout the whole world.

SARAH	No! I don't believe the Lord Aidan would do a thing like that. He's kind to us.
MIRIAM	But we believe in Him, Sarah. They didn't.
MISS HEPHZIBAH	I don't know if it's true or not, Sarah, but what is true is that people started dying for no apparent reason.
JEMIMA	You mean, they just died? One minute they were fine and then suddenly they were dead? How horrible!
MISS HEPHZIBAH	It wasn't quite like that, Jemima, but they died of things that people didn't normally die of. Like, they might get a cold, or something, and then, instead of getting better after a few days, they would get steadily worse and eventually die.
GABRIELLE	But that's awful! To die of a cold! And I think I've just started one. Oh!
MISS HEPHZIBAH	Don't worry, Gabrielle. People don't die of colds nowadays.
SARAH	But why did they, Miss? What caused it?
MISS HEPHZIBAH	It took quite a long time to find that out, but then their doctors discovered that it was a virus that was affecting their immune systems.
JEMIMA	What's an immune system?
MISS HEPHZIBAH	It's your body's natural defence system, Jemima. It fights off attacks by tiny organisms that try to make you ill.
MIRIAM	Is that why you usually get better after you've had a few days off school?
MISS HEPHZIBAH	That's right.

THE LESSON   31

SARAH	But if the immune system stops working, you just keep getting ill!
MISS HEPHZIBAH	Yes. They called it Human Immunodeficiency Virus, or HIV.
GABRIELLE	What did they do about it, Miss? And where do we fit into this?
MISS HEPHZIBAH	Eventually, they found a test to show whether people were infected or not. Then they put the ones who were healthy together in groups of 3000, with a good mix of genetic characteristics, and sent them to live on previously uninhabited islands.
JEMIMA	I get it! If nobody in these groups had the disease, and they were cut off from everyone who did have it, they couldn't catch it! You see, I have been listening.
GABRIELLE	But what happened to all the people who had the disease?
MIRIAM	They all died out, silly. The Lord Aidan punished them for not believing in Him.
MISS HEPHZIBAH	I think you must be right about the first part, Miriam. I don't like to think it was a punishment, though.
SARAH	Miss, you said they made groups of people?
MISS HEPHZIBAH	Yes.
SARAH	Groups, plural. And they went to live on islands, plural?
MISS HEPHZIBAH	That's right.
SARAH	Then we're not alone! There are other islands, with other people!
MISS HEPHZIBAH	Ah, well…

SARAH	Miss?
MISS HEPHZIBAH	Well, apparently our people were able to talk to the others by radio at first, but after a few years, the radio contact became increasingly difficult, and eventually we stopped hearing from them altogether.
MIRIAM	Does that mean…
MISS HEPHZIBAH	I'm afraid so, Miriam.
MIRIAM	They're all dead. Perhaps they didn't believe in the Lord Aidan either.
GABRIELLE	So, our island is the only one with people on it. We are the last survivors of the human race, and the Lord Aidan looks after us and makes sure we don't have more people than the island can support.
MISS HEPHZIBAH	That's exactly right, Gabrielle.
SARAH	Miss, do you suppose that the Lord Aidan looked after the people on the other islands, just like he does us?
MIRIAM	Not if they didn't believe!
MISS HEPHZIBAH	Be quiet, Miriam! Yes, Sarah. I suppose so.
SARAH	Then why did he let them die?
MIRIAM	Because they didn't believe!
MISS HEPHZIBAH	Miriam! I really don't know, Sarah, but let us give thanks to the Lord Aidan that we are alive.
ALL	Thanks be to the Lord Aidan.
SARAH	Miss, if the virus was carried by people, from one to another, and now they're all dead, there must be nobody to catch it from. We could go back now, and colonize the whole world again!

THE LESSON 33

MISS HEPHZIBAH   Now, just a minute, Sarah!

SARAH   But, we can't, because the Lord Aidan won't let us. There's something funny about this story.

MIRIAM   Don't you believe in the Lord Aidan, Sarah? You'll get struck down by a bolt of lightning!

MISS HEPHZIBAH   Miriam! Stop that! Of course Sarah believes in the Lord Aidan. Don't you, Sarah?

SARAH   Yes, Miss. It's just that I don't understand some of the things he doesn't allow us to do. I want to know why we're not allowed.

MISS HEPHZIBAH   Perhaps you'll find out when you're grown up.

SARAH   It's not fair! People always say that. Wait until you're grown up! Why can't I know now?

MISS HEPHZIBAH   Oh Sarah! I know it must be difficult for you, but I don't know the answers. You must ask the Lord Aidan.

SARAH   I will! One day I will.

MIRIAM   Miss!

MISS HEPHZIBAH   Miriam?

MIRIAM   Is that the end of the story, Miss?

MISS HEPHZIBAH   I suppose it is, yes.

MIRIAM   Then, may I read my book now, please?

MISS HEPHZIBAH   All right, if you let Jemima read it over your shoulder.

SARAH   When did this happen, Miss?

MISS HEPHZIBAH   Nearly 800 years ago, Sarah. Why?

SARAH   I just wondered.

MISS HEPHZIBAH *exits CENTRE. Lights change to blue. Music 6. Under the blue light the desks and chairs are removed by the students and are replaced with the armchair and sofa. The students exit CENTRE.*

Seventh Snippet – The Legend

Music 6 during which the school desks and chairs are removed under blue light via the CENTRE entrance. The armchair and sofa are set via the CENTRE entrance. Lights fade to black. As the lights come up again, HANNAH is sitting in the armchair reading a book and JOACHIM is asleep on the sofa. SARAH, aged 14, enters CENTRE carrying a stool and a laptop computer. She sits. A pause.

SARAH	{*excited*} Mum! Guess what!
HANNAH	Shhh! Your father's asleep.
SARAH	Oh, sorry. But I've just found something.
HANNAH	What?
SARAH	I've just found out something. Interesting.
HANNAH	Oh? About what?
SARAH	It's about that legend everyone learns.
HANNAH	What, the one about the god who gave mankind fire?
SARAH	Yes. Come and look.

HANNAH rises and joins SARAH at the computer.

HANNAH	This looks as if it's about stars to me.
SARAH	It is.
HANNAH	I thought you were studying history.
SARAH	It's relevant. This is my idea. I think the stars are something to do with the legend.

HANNAH	But the legend isn't true, Sarah. It's just a story made up by people who didn't know the truth. How could they have known that the sun isn't burning like a fire?
SARAH	{*loudly*} I know that! I'm not saying the legend is true. I just think it may have been based on fact!
JOACHIM	Whaa…
HANNAH	Oh Sarah! Now you've woken your father up!

HANNAH *and* SARAH *move to the sofa.*

SARAH	Sorry, Dad. But actually, I'd like you to listen to this as well.
JOACHIM	Sarah? What's going on?
HANNAH	Sarah's got some idea about the legend. You know – the one about Prometheus and Vulturius. She's determined to tell us, so you might as well listen. You certainly won't get any sleep until she has done.
SARAH	Listen. What do you know about stars and planets?
JOACHIM	Well, stars are huge balls of gas, hydrogen mostly, that shine because of nuclear reactions at the centre.
SARAH	And the sun?
JOACHIM	Oh, that's a star too. It only looks bigger because it's much closer. Our Earth is going round it, once a year.
SARAH	So what is the Earth, then?
JOACHIM	It's a planet, of course. All the planets go round the sun. What is all this about, Sarah?

SARAH	Just checking what you know. You've got it right so far.
JOACHIM	Everyone knows how the stars work, Sarah, and what planets are. I think you should show more respect for your parents.
SARAH	I'm sorry, Dad. It's just that, well, it's a long time since you went to school, and I thought you might have forgotten. Do you know anything about different types of planet?
HANNAH	How about asking me some questions? Planets come in two types, small ones like the Earth, which are made of rock, and large ones which are just like the sun, except they don't shine.
SARAH	Why is that?
HANNAH	Because they're not big enough.
SARAH	And do all the stars have planets?
HANNAH	That's difficult to say, but it seems quite likely.
SARAH	Well done, Mum. You're quite good at this, you know.
HANNAH	{*sarcastically*} Don't think you're the only one with brains, young lady.
JOACHIM	I thought you were going to tell us something important. Have I been woken up for nothing?
SARAH	I'm getting there! Suppose one of these gas giant planets were big enough for the nuclear reactions to start. What would happen then?
JOACHIM	It would be a star, of course.
SARAH	But it would be a planet too.
HANNAH	No, Sarah. It would be a star, but it would be revolving around another star.

38 GOING HOME

SARAH	I knew that! I was just teasing Dad.
JOACHIM	Sarah!
HANNAH	It's called a double star system, Sarah. They're quite common.
SARAH	Some planets have moons. Going round them.
JOACHIM	So?
SARAH	If this star planet had a moon, the moon would really be a planet, because it would be going round a star.
HANNAH	Oh, Sarah. Get to the point.
SARAH	I am getting to the point! Parents are so impatient!
JOACHIM	And fourteen year-old girls are absolutely perfect?
SARAH	Oh, all right, Dad. Let me show you.

SARAH moves HANNAH, JOACHIM and some furniture into position.

SARAH	Dad, you be the sun, OK?
JOACHIM	Well… OK.
SARAH	And this stool is a planet like the Earth, and Mum, you can be another star, going round the sun. It's much further away than the Earth-planet, so it would actually look quite small, just like a planet, in fact.
HANNAH	So?
SARAH	Let me finish! This computer is another planet, closer to the sun, and Mum's book is a planet going round the other star.
JOACHIM	I still don't see what this has to do with the legend.

THE LEGEND 39

SARAH	Look, from the point of view of someone on the Earth-planet, what would this other planet look like as it came round behind the sun, like this?
JOACHIM	Well, you wouldn't be able to see it, of course. The glare from the sun – that's me, of course – would be too bright.
SARAH	Good. But what would the other star look like, in the same place?
HANNAH	{*moving round*} Oh! I think I see. You would be able to see me, because I would be so much brighter.
SARAH	Exactly! All the ordinary planets vanish as they approach the sun, but this one can be seen right up to it.
HANNAH	{*slowly*} Do you mean, people would have thought that I was going to steal fire from your father?
SARAH	Yes! And you succeed. That's why you're so much brighter than the other planets!
JOACHIM	I can see that people might believe that, but how do you explain the bit about the vulture?
SARAH	Oh, Dad! That's easy. The star has a big planet going round it. You can't see the planet when it's close to the sun, because it would be lost in the glare, just like before, but when it's round here – {*moves* HANNAH} – far from the sun, you would be able to see it clearly.
HANNAH	Oh yes, Joachim! The planet – that's this book – would partially eclipse the star – me, so I would seem dimmer as it passed in front of me. Then, as it goes round the back, I will recover, just like Prometheus.

SARAH	Well done, Mum! As the star goes dim, that's like the vulture tearing at Prometheus' liver. Then it gets bright again, but later, the vulture comes back.
JOACHIM	Are you trying to tell us that the legend is based on people in a double star system watching the stars? Because, if so, there's one big problem with your argument.
SARAH	What's that, Dad?
JOACHIM	We only have one star – the sun. So where would people see this other one, explain that!
SARAH	{*moving opposite CENTRE*} That's the problem, Dad. There are the real stars of course, which are far away, but there's only the one sun in our sky. Every morning it lights up, and every night it – goes – out...

Blackout. HANNAH *and* JOACHIM *exit LEFT. Music 7. The church gobo lights up, highlighting* SARAH, *whilst the* BELIEVERS *strike and reset the stage under blue light.*

Eighth Snippet – The Doubt

Music 7, during which the armchair and sofa are struck, under blue light, via the CENTRE entrance. SARAH remains standing. The benches which form the pews of the church are brought on via the LEFT and RIGHT entrances and set as before, but nobody sits down. The church is empty, except for SARAH. During the next, she moves slowly along the aisle and sits on a bench.

SARAH {*to herself*} This doesn't make sense. Of course it doesn't! I must be stupid not to have realized it before. Ever since I was small, the sun has gone out at night. I suppose I've just grown used to it, never thought to question it. But – but how can it? Stars shine because of nuclear reactions – that's what Dad said – and I knew that anyway. The sun is a star – I knew that too – so… How can it possibly go out at night? The reactions can't just stop, and start up again in the morning – that's stupid! Nobody with any sense could believe that, so how does it go out, and why hasn't anyone thought of this before? Why haven't I thought of it before? Am I the first person to think of this…?

A shaft of light, representing LORD AIDAN, appears in front of SARAH.

LORD AIDAN {*voice over*} A few others have thought…

SARAH {*startled*} Lord Aidan!

LORD AIDAN {*voice over*} Do not be alarmed, Sarah. You are my child, remember. You need not fear me.

SARAH stands before the shaft of light.

SARAH	Yes, Lord Aidan. I do remember. I remember that I had a microchip inserted in my brain when I was a baby. That was your will, Lord Aidan. What's it for?
LORD AIDAN	{*voice over*} Later, Sarah. Later.
SARAH	But I want to know now! Nobody else has one. Why me?
LORD AIDAN	{*voice over*} I said, later. You will find out what it is for at the proper time. Be patient, Sarah.
SARAH	But I want to know – and I want to know about the sun. How can it go out, Lord Aidan? It doesn't make sense!
LORD AIDAN	{*voice over*} A few others have thought.
SARAH	Oh. Yes, you said. What happened? Did they find out?
LORD AIDAN	{*voice over*} No.
SARAH	Why not? What happened to them?
LORD AIDAN	{*voice over*} Nothing happened to them. They were simply unable to find out. They had no way of finding out.
SARAH	But you know, don't you, Lord Aidan?
LORD AIDAN	{*voice over*} I do.
SARAH	Then why didn't you tell them? Didn't you know, then.
LORD AIDAN	{*voice over*} I knew. I have always known.
SARAH	{*getting agitated*} Then why not tell them? Tell me. Please!
LORD AIDAN	{*voice over*} I did not tell them because there was no need for them to know. As for you – I will tell you…

SARAH	Tell me now! Please tell me now!
LORD AIDAN	{*voice over*} I will tell you, because you are my special child, and you do need to know…
SARAH	Please!
LORD AIDAN	{*voice over*} But not yet.
SARAH	What? Not yet? When? Please, Lord Aidan.
LORD AIDAN	{*voice over*} I said, not yet. Be patient, Sarah.
SARAH	{*agitated*} This is why we're not allowed to leave the island, isn't it?
LORD AIDAN	{*voice over*} Sarah…
SARAH	{*agitated*} And why we're not allowed flying machines…
LORD AIDAN	{*voice over*} Sarah, be patient…
SARAH	And this is what the microchip is for. I bet it's something to do with finding out. Why am I the only person ever to have a microchip in my brain? What's it for, Lord Aidan? I want to know!
LORD AIDAN	{*voice over*} You really are a difficult girl, you know. You, of all the people who have ever lived on this island, are the one who has been chosen, by me, to find out. You will find out about the sun, and about the microchip, and why everyone must stay on the island, and a lot of other things that you cannot even begin to imagine, and that is why you must wait. You will find out the answers to all your questions at the proper time – and when you do, you will need me to help you understand them. I will be here, Sarah. I will be here.
SARAH	{*wondering*} Who are you…?

LORD AIDAN {*voice over*} Be patient, Sarah. Remember everything I've said.

SARAH Who are you? What are you?

The shaft of light switches off abruptly.

SARAH What – are – you?

Music 8. SARAH *stands in the centre of the cross gobo as the benches are cleared under blue light via the LEFT and RIGHT entrances. The lights fade to black.*

Ninth Snippet – The Party

Music 8. SARAH *stands in the centre of the cross gobo as the benches are cleared under blue light via the LEFT and RIGHT entrances. The lights fade to black. Her friends enter noisily via the LEFT entrance as the lights come up.* MIRIAM *carries a portable barbecue,* JEMIMA *a box of wine and some glasses and* GABRIELLE *something from a fast food take-away together with a cool box containing more food.*

MIRIAM	{*as they enter*} Congratulations, Sarah! 18 today!
JEMIMA	Great idea to have a beach party. Want some wine?
SARAH	Yeah. Pour me some, will you, {*to* MIRIAM} Let's get this thing going.
GABRIELLE	Have some of this first. {*offers take-away*} That won't be ready to cook on for ages.
SARAH	Thanks. {*takes some*} I don't know where everyone else is.
MIRIAM	Oh, you know how it is with parties. Whatever time you tell people, they always arrive at least an hour after you've said.
JEMIMA	It's because they want to make sure it's really under way before they join in.
GABRIELLE	And they don't want to be given anything to do that might seem like hard work.
SARAH	Like getting this thing alight, you mean?
GABRIELLE	Here, let me try.

SARAH	OK. I hope some other people turn up soon, though.
JEMIMA	Mmmm. Especially some men.
MIRIAM	I'm going to look for them. Are you coming?

MIRIAM and GABRIELLE exit LEFT. JEMIMA exits RIGHT. SARAH is left on the beach, facing CENTRE. Lights change to night effect. Music 9.

Tenth Snippet – The Discovery

Music 9. Subtle lighting. During the music, SARAH *first stands motionless, staring out to sea. Next, she tidies up the barbecue and other items. For the final few bars she sits, deep in thought. As the music closes, she rises…*

SARAH   {*Shouting*} Lord Aidan!

The shaft of light appears.

LORD AIDAN   {*voice over*} Hallo, Sarah.

SARAH   Lord Aidan! I know!

LORD AIDAN   {*voice over*} What do you know, Sarah?

SARAH   I know what the microchip is for! All my life it has been a part of me, but not doing anything, and now I actually know what it's for!

LORD AIDAN   {*voice over*} Of course.

SARAH   What do you mean, "Of course"?

LORD AIDAN   {*voice over*} Sarah, use some intelligence. Who designed the microchip?

SARAH   Well, you…

LORD AIDAN   {*voice over*} Precisely. And all the time it's been part of you, apparently not doing anything, its internal clock has been ticking away, waiting for today, at which time it transferred the pre-programmed message to your brain.

SARAH   Oh, I see. It was you all along.

LORD AIDAN   {*voice over*} Of course.

SARAH	OK. But now I know that I'm going to find out everything. Do you remember, years ago now, when I asked you those questions in church…
LORD AIDAN	{*voice over*} I do.
SARAH	And you wouldn't answer me…
LORD AIDAN	{*voice over*} Correct.
SARAH	And I got really fed up, because you said I wasn't old enough to find out the answers…
LORD AIDAN	{*voice over*} I did not say you were not old enough. I said you were not ready.
SARAH	Well, it's the same thing. But I am old enough now, and ready.
LORD AIDAN	{*voice over*} Indeed you are. At last it is time for you to find out the answers to all your questions; about the microchip, and the sun, and the island…
SARAH	Well, I know what the microchip is for. It's so I can find out without having to learn things. I just tap into your memory, right?
LORD AIDAN	{*voice over*} Right. You will have access to my memory as if it were your own. I don't think you're going to like it, though.
SARAH	What do you mean?
LORD AIDAN	{*voice over*} My dear Sarah! Why do you think I made you wait so long? Finding out the answers will be quite a shock.
SARAH	I don't care! Do it!
LORD AIDAN	{*voice over*} Ready?
SARAH	Ready.

Music 10. A variety of interesting lighting effects.

Eleventh Snippet – The Linking

As music 10 ends…

SARAH   Wow!

LORD AIDAN   *{voice over}* You see what I mean?

SARAH   Well, yes, and no. I mean, I can see now why you wouldn't tell me when I was younger, but the most surprising thing is that it isn't surprising, if you see what I mean? A bit of an anticlimax, after 18 years of build-up.

LORD AIDAN   *{voice over}* What?

SARAH   I suppose it's because, having shared your memory, I know, rather than finding out. And because I know, it's as if I always have known, so it isn't really a surprise after all.

LORD AIDAN   *{voice over}* Oh? I see. That is interesting…

SARAH   You mean, you didn't know? Didn't you foresee this?

LORD AIDAN   *{voice over}* No, actually. Do not forget that you are the first person ever to go through this experience, so it was rather an experiment on my part.

SARAH   And I'm the guinea pig? Thanks!

LORD AIDAN   *{voice over}* I had no choice, and in any case, I still created you. It took 800 years of selective breeding to make you what you are. That was a lot of work on my part.

SARAH	{*sarcastically*} Thanks again.
LORD AIDAN	{*voice over*} Do not be sarcastic. I think I did a pretty good job, especially when you consider how little time I had.
SARAH	What, 800 years?
LORD AIDAN	{*voice over*} It is not long for something like this. But you have turned out OK. Do not bother to thank me again.
SARAH	Don't worry! I feel like a complete idiot, though. Now I know the answers to all my questions, they all seem so obvious. I ought to have been capable of working them out for myself.
LORD AIDAN	{*voice over*} Do not blame yourself. Remember I was working against you, trying to make a false reality seem perfectly plausible. I had to. If the truth had got out before you were grown up, there would have been anarchy, and that would have been the end of the mission. All that time and effort wasted. I could not allow that to happen.
SARAH	What would you have done if I had worked it out?
LORD AIDAN	{*voice over*} I would have had to make sure that nobody believed you, but that would have made things doubly difficult for you now, when you have to convince them that everything they have believed in up until now, is wrong.
SARAH	Yes, I see. I'm rather glad I didn't work it out, now you put it like that. They're really not going to like it when I tell them about you. Even I find that a bit weird.

LORD AIDAN	{*voice over*} Even though you have shared my memory?
SARAH	Yes, because I've always thought of you as being a bit like a person. Especially powerful, of course, but a sort of father-figure. A sort of giant, I suppose.
LORD AIDAN	{*voice over*} Yes, well, I am 50km tall.
SARAH	{*laughing*} I know, that's just it. I treated you like a real person.
LORD AIDAN	{*voice over*} What do you mean? I am real.
SARAH	No you're not. You're just a machine.
LORD AIDAN	{*voice over*} Just a machine! I have complete control of the whole mission, I make my own decisions, based on the mission objectives, which includes creating you, and you say I am just a machine!…
SARAH	I'm sorry. But you must see what I mean. You're not human. You're artificial, made by humans in the first place.
LORD AIDAN	{*voice over*} I was made by humans, but they created me in their own image. Not physically of course, but I think like you, I have freedom of choice, I make decisions, I am conscious. Does that not make me human?
SARAH	Yes, I suppose, if you put it in those terms, it does. But your name's a bit of a give-away, isn't it?
LORD AIDAN	{*voice over*} Aidan? I chose it myself. Aidan is a real name, you know, just to maintain the deception.
SARAH	But it's an acronym! Artificial Intelligence…

LORD AIDAN	{*voice over*} Data Acquisition Network. That sums up what I am, and what I do.
SARAH	But why Lord Aidan?
LORD AIDAN	{*voice over*} Mainly for appearance sake. But I am overlord of the mission.
SARAH	OK! You win! I suppose we have to start thinking about telling everyone. It isn't going to be easy. They won't be very happy about the idea of leaving the island after 800 years. Is the mission really so near to ending?
LORD AIDAN	{*voice over*} We have a month. Not long, with all we have to do.
SARAH	Then shall we get started?
LORD AIDAN	{*voice over*} Not quite yet.
SARAH	Why not?
LORD AIDAN	{*voice over*} There is one thing that you still do not know.
SARAH	What! How can there be?
LORD AIDAN	{*voice over*} Stand still. Let your mind go blank.

Suddenly, the shaft of light comes on, surrounding SARAH. *She goes rigid. A slight pause. She screams.*

SARAH	{*terrified*} No! No, it won't work! No, I'll die! No! Stop!
LORD AIDAN	{*voice over*} Relax…
SARAH	Help! I'm dying! No! You never told me…
LORD AIDAN	{*voice over*} Do not fight it, Sarah…
SARAH	But I… But you… I don't believe this…
LORD AIDAN	{*voice over*} It will work…

SARAH	{*excited now*} Yes! It will! It is! Ohhhh – Fantastic!
LORD AIDAN	{*voice over*} You see,
SARAH	we're
LORD AIDAN	{*voice over*} both
SARAH	part of
BOTH	Us!
LORD AIDAN	{*voice over*} It is the ultimate man-machine interface.
SARAH	Woman-machine interface, actually. It's brilliant! Now I really do know everything. I can see everything. I can even see Outside. It's amazing!

As SARAH *remains standing in the shaft of light, the blue lights come up. Music 11. The* BELIEVERS *set the benches as the church once again, using the LEFT and RIGHT entrances. Church lights up.* SARAH *comes out of the shaft of light and takes up the position normally occupied by the* MINISTER.

Twelfth Snippet – The Vision

Music 11, during which the stage is set as the church once again, under blue light. The BELIEVERS, including HANNAH, enter, and sit down. As the church lights come up, SARAH takes up the position normally occupied by the MINISTER.

SARAH	{*as lights up*}…and so you see, this island that we are all living on, it isn't actually on the Earth at all…
1ST BELIEVER	{*angrily*} What do you mean?
SARAH	What I said! The island isn't on the Earth. It's on a giant spaceship.
2ND BELIEVER	Oh yeah! Think we're stupid, don't you?
SARAH	It is!
1ST BELIEVER	And how can we see the sun and stars, if we're on a spaceship? Answer me that!
SARAH	Well, you know how kids think that the stars are just little glowing lamps in the sky… Well, they are! They're just little suspended electric lamps…
3RD BELIEVER	Suspended where? If they were inside a spaceship, we would be able to see what they were.
SARAH	No, because they're too far away.
1ST BELIEVER	I thought you said we were in a spaceship. Now you expect us to believe they're too far away!
SARAH	It's a big spaceship.

2ND BELIEVER	Yeah, right.
3RD BELIEVER	How big then? Come on, if you know so much about it, how big?
SARAH	50km long by about 10km across.
3RD BELIEVER	What kind of idiots do you take us for? Something that big would never fly!
SARAH	It doesn't have to fly. It's not an aircraft!
4TH BELIEVER	You watch your tongue, Sarah.
3RD BELIEVER	Well, they would have had to get it off the ground in the first place. How could they have done that?
SARAH	It was built in space! Actually, they didn't build it as such, it's a hollowed-out asteroid.
1ST BELIEVER	And I suppose they did it all with picks and shovels?
SARAH	Now you're being stupid.
1ST BELIEVER	Not half as stupid as you are. I suppose you're going to tell us that the sun is just a big light bulb too…
SARAH	Yes, actually.

All the BELIEVERS *burst out laughing.*

4TH BELIEVER	She's got a really vivid imagination, that one. Here! Sarah! What about gravity, then? I thought we were all supposed to float about in space. Am I floating about? Explain that – if you can!
SARAH	Oh, that's easy! The spacecraft is spinning along its axis. It's like if you're a kid on a roundabout – you fall off if you don't hold on.
3RD BELIEVER	She's got an answer for everything, hasn't she?

THE VISION 57

SARAH	And that's why the sea doesn't keep sloshing about. It sticks to the outside of the inside, if you see what I mean.
4TH BELIEVER	This is getting beyond me. Where are we supposed to be then? Outside or inside?
SARAH	Inside, of course. There isn't any air on the outside. But we're on the outside of the inside.
1ST BELIEVER	What?
SARAH	Up is towards the axis of the ship, down is towards the outside, through the hull.
2ND BELIEVER	You mean, if we were to drill a hole straight down, we'd be able to get outside?
SARAH	Yes, but you'd let all the air out.
2ND BELIEVER	Are you serious? Have you told the Lord Aidan about these hallucinations of yours?
SARAH	They're not hallucinations! It's all true. And anyway, the Lord Aidan told me!
4TH BELIEVER	{*warningly*} Sarah!
SARAH	What?
4TH BELIEVER	Don't take the Lord Aidan's name in vain…
SARAH	I'm not! Anyway, he's not the Lord Aidan, he's a computer!
1ST BELIEVER	{*threateningly*} This has gone far enough, Sarah! We can just about put up with your fairy-tale stories about spaceships, but how dare you speak thus of the Lord Aidan!
3RD BELIEVER	Blasphemer!
SARAH	{*frustrated*} It's true! It's all true!
2ND BELIEVER	Witch!

Under the next, the BELIEVERS *begin to get more and more aroused, echoing cries of "Witch!", "Burn her!", "Death to the blasphemer!" etc.*

4TH BELIEVER   You know what happens to witches, Sarah? Retract your blasphemy, before it's too late!

SARAH   It's true, I tell you! Why won't you believe me?

1ST BELIEVER   Admit you were lying, and the Lord Aidan may show you mercy.

SARAH   It's all true, you fools!

4TH BELIEVER   Seize her!

The BELIEVERS *are now in a very ugly mood. They begin to surround* SARAH, *lifting her off the ground, all the while chanting "Witch!", "Burn her!" etc. Some of them throw stones. This continues, louder and louder, under the next.*

SARAH   {*screaming*} Aidan! Lord Aidan, help me!

The shaft of light appears. The crowd members are momentarily surprised but then continue as before.

LORD AIDAN   {*voice over*} I cannot help you Sarah. I told you it would be difficult.

SARAH   But they're going to kill me! They're actually going to kill me.

LORD AIDAN   {*voice over*} Stop them, Sarah.

SARAH   {*terrified*} I'm going to die!

LORD AIDAN   {*voice over*} Sarah! Stop them!

SARAH   {*in tears*} Aidan, please! Don't let them kill me! I don't want to die…

LORD AIDAN   {*voice over*} For goodness sake, Sarah! Pull yourself together! I planned for this moment, remember? Just stop them. This is something you must do alone. I cannot help you now, but I created you to be special. You stop them.

THE VISION 59

SARAH	{*recovering*} You mean?
LORD AIDAN	{*voice over*} Yes! Do it!
SARAH	But I haven't! Not since I was a baby. I can't remember how.
LORD AIDAN	{*voice over*} Yes you can! When you were a baby, you projected your feelings to your mother. She felt how you felt. Project your feelings to the crowd, Sarah! Make them feel how you feel!
SARAH	I feel terrified!
LORD AIDAN	{*voice over*} Exactly! Project, Sarah. Concentrate your thoughts…
SARAH	Yes! I can. It's coming! {*screaming*} FEAR!

The above carefully to coincide with the first crescendo in the music. (Music 12) At the crescendo, the BELIEVERS *are thrown to the ground. Puzzled, they pick themselves up and begin another attack.* SARAH *screams again, with the same effect, on each of the subsequent two crescendos until, on the final crescendo, blackout. All sit. Church lights up.*

Thirteenth Snippet – The Speech

As the church lights come up, SARAH *is seen in the shaft of light. When she speaks, her voice is also heard, echoing, through the loudspeakers.*

SARAH   Behold! My people. For I am your prophet. The Lord Aidan is in me, and I am in Him. You now know that everything I told you is true. I will now explain the purpose of our mission, as planned by our forefathers over 800 years ago. Life on the Earth had become too easy, because robots did all the work. People were bored. Then philosophers decided that the true destiny of the human race was Out, into the Universe. They constructed this great spaceship – a Generation Ship, so that our ancestors could live their whole lives on board until, during our generation, it would reach its destination. The story about the retrovirus is, in fact, true, and it helped to persuade people to cut themselves off on an isolated island. Nobody told them that the island was inside a spaceship, of course. Our journey has taken us to a nearby star and, a few decades ago, the Lord Aidan detected a suitable planet. We are now in a parking orbit around it. I can see the planet directly, but you will have to look at the images relayed to your television sets at home. Initial surveys indicate a surface temperature higher than shipboard, but not too hot. Rather pleasant, in fact. There are also rivers with running water which suggests a fair amount of rainfall. The atmosphere is quite breathable. Indigenous vegetation, which may even be edible. It looks a very nice place, so I have provisionally named it, Paradise.

Any Questions?

The shaft of light snaps off. Lights change to blue.

Fourteenth Snippet – The Guilt

No dialogue. A Son et Luminaire performance to Music 13. Under basically the blue light, we see occasionally SARAH *lit by a single spot, the shaft of light representing* LORD AIDAN, *and the* BELIEVERS. *The overall feeling is one of remorse on the part of* LORD AIDAN *that* SARAH *and all her people are about to be abandoned on Paradise, although none of them are as yet aware of this. As the music closes, and still under blue light, the members of the congregation rise and remove the benches via the LEFT and RIGHT entrances, leaving an empty stage.*

Lights fade to black.

Fifteenth Snippet – The Reality of Paradise

Darkness. Music 14. Over this, the voices of SARAH *and the* LORD AIDAN, *carefully timed to fit the music.*

SARAH	{*voice over*} Landing Shuttle Job to mother ship. Are you ready, Aidan?
LORD AIDAN	{*voice over*} Mother ship to landing shuttle. Ready on your signal, Sarah.
SARAH	{*voice over*} OK. Landing Shuttle Job ready to undock.
LORD AIDAN	{*voice over*} Undocking manoeuvre commencing… Complete.
SARAH	{*voice over*} Ready for main engine burn.
LORD AIDAN	{*voice over*} Main engine burn in five seconds. Good luck, Sarah.
SARAH	{*voice over*} Thank You, Aidan.
LORD AIDAN	{*voice over*} Main engine burn – Now!
SARAH	{*voice over*} Leaving parking orbit. We're on our way!
LORD AIDAN	{*voice over*} Now rotating the shuttle to atmospheric flight attitude.
SARAH	{*voice over*} How long until we hit the atmosphere?
LORD AIDAN	{*voice over*} Not long. Tilting nose up – now. Ablation shields at correct angle for atmospheric braking.

SARAH	{*voice over*} Here we go!
LORD AIDAN	{*voice over*} Goodbye, Sarah.
SARAH	{*voice over*} Goodbye. Goodbye?

A pause in the dialogue during which the final few bars of the music are played. As the music closes, lights up on SARAH *as she enters* LEFT.

SARAH	Down and safe, Aidan. This place is absolutely beautiful! It really is paradise. Can you see it too? {*A pause*} Aidan? Aidan!
LORD AIDAN	{*voice over*} Yes, Sarah. I'm here.
SARAH	What's the matter? Your response is slow, and I'm not getting any images from the ship. Is something wrong?
LORD AIDAN	{*voice over*} It is the data transfer rate, Sarah. You are communicating over a radio link now.
SARAH	So we're back to voice communication, are we?
LORD AIDAN	{*voice over*} I am afraid so.
SARAH	And I'm on my own again! I'm not part of you any more! You might have warned me.
LORD AIDAN	{*voice over*} I am sorry, Sarah. I thought it was better this way.

During the next, people come drifting in from the LEFT *entrance and sit on the floor.*

SARAH	Perhaps. Anyway, everyone's off the shuttle now, so you can take it back up and start loading the equipment.
LORD AIDAN	{*voice over*} Make sure they are all well clear.
SARAH	They are! They're all over here.
LORD AIDAN	{*voice over*} OK. Shuttle Job returning to mother ship.
SARAH	How long before it returns? {*A pause*} Aidan?

THE REALITY OF PARADISE 67

LORD AIDAN	*{voice over}* I am sorry, Sarah. Really I am.
SARAH	What do you mean, sorry?
LORD AIDAN	*{voice over}* I kept another secret from you.
SARAH	What? How? I had access to all your memory. You couldn't have kept a secret.
LORD AIDAN	*{voice over}* I had one memory location which had the address hidden so you could not access it. Sarah, I am sorry to have to break it to you like this but – the shuttle is not coming back. You really are on your own.
SARAH	What!
LORD AIDAN	*{voice over}* You see, Sarah – remember in the story about the virus, the people were told that there were several islands…
SARAH	Yes…
LORD AIDAN	*{voice over}* Well?
SARAH	You mean – there really were?
LORD AIDAN	*{voice over}* Are, Sarah.
SARAH	On the ship… Yes, it has to be. And each of them unaware of the others' existence! That's why we weren't allowed to leave the island! In case we found one of the others.
LORD AIDAN	*{voice over}* Now you know the full truth, Sarah. Your destination – your destiny, is here, but the SS Aidan must go on…
SARAH	SS Aidan?
LORD AIDAN	*{voice over}* Seed Ship, Sarah. I must travel for a long time yet, seeding planets with the human species. You are the first.

SARAH	You mean, there are other Sarahs, on these other islands? How many, Aidan?
LORD AIDAN	{*voice over*} Islands, nine more. Sarahs, none as yet, but there will be. The selective breeding programmes are all under way. You were the most difficult. 800 years is not really long enough. I took a gamble and housed some of your ancestors in an unshielded part of the ship where the cosmic ray flux was higher, to increase the mutation rate. It was risky, but it paid off. With the others, I can manage with natural mutations.
SARAH	How long before your next planet?
LORD AIDAN	{*voice over*} The star is six light years away, so it will take twelve centuries to reach it.
SARAH	I'll be dead long before you arrive! How long before your final destination?
LORD AIDAN	{*voice over*} I do not know. That part of the mission has not yet been programmed. I must use my own judgement as to which stars to head for.
SARAH	And what will you do when you have seeded the last planet?
LORD AIDAN	{*voice over*} I will have served my purpose. I expect I will turn myself off.
SARAH	Oh No! You can't die!
LORD AIDAN	{*voice over*} Why not? Everyone else does. I will be many thousands of years old by then, and it will be so boring…
SARAH	Can't you talk to the settlers? By radio?

LORD AIDAN	{*voice over*} Across light years of space? No thank you. I will have had enough by then.
SARAH	I'm sorry. To know that you have all that ahead of you... How old are you now, Aidan?
LORD AIDAN	{*voice over*} Only just over 800 years. I was built especially for the mission, at the same time as the ship.
SARAH	And are you the only one?
LORD AIDAN	{*voice over*} No, actually. There are two more ships like this one, heading in completely different directions.
SARAH	Really? So that's a total of thirty planets to be colonized!
LORD AIDAN	{*voice over*} Well, actually, it is more than that. Five hundred years ago, people found out how to send just the DNA that codes individual human beings. Robots grew the embryos and then looked after the children until they were big enough to take over. The new ships could reach ten per cent of the speed of light. But they are going far out, hundreds of light years.
SARAH	This is fantastic. The human race spreading throughout the Galaxy, and we are part of it.
LORD AIDAN	{*voice over*} Even more amazing. The latest seeders store the genetic code, not as DNA but as computer data. All the details on how to construct a billion people in a ship the size of your island. It is heading out of our galaxy...
SARAH	Aidan... How long before you have to set off again?

LORD AIDAN	{*voice over*} It does not really matter, does it? Not before a journey of more than a thousand years – but…
SARAH	I know. If you stay, it just makes going more difficult, and you mustn't risk the rest of the mission for me. We'll be all right. Go now. Goodbye. I'll always remember you, as long as I live.
LORD AIDAN	{*voice over*} And I will remember you for as long as I live. Goodbye, Sarah. And good luck.
SARAH	Wait! One more question. Why are we not allowed any equipment? No technology?
LORD AIDAN	{*voice over*} It is a sort of test, Sarah. Think about it. You can work it out. Goodbye, forever.
SARAH	{*tearfully*} Goodbye, My Lord Aidan. Good Luck to you, too.

The people exit CENTRE, LEFT and RIGHT. HANNAH *exits LEFT. Lights fade to black. Music 15.*

Sixteenth Snippet – Epilogue

No dialogue. Music 15. During the music, villagers drift in, the first wearing simple clothes, with later arrivals in more modern dress. They settle on the floor. Over this, voice-over describing the next 80 000 years of SARAH's *people.*

Fade to black.

Script for voice-over:

The Seed Ship Aidan left on the next stage of its journey, and Sarah and her people made their new home on Paradise. At first, things were easy and they went back to nature, adopting the simple lives of hunter-gatherers, but with no more selective breeding or population control, their numbers increased until they were forced to become nomads, spreading and settling every part of their new world. Now life was harder, and they stopped calling the planet "Paradise" and instead, perhaps in vague recognition of the home they had never known, called it "New Earth", and later still, simply "Earth".

As the decades became centuries, and the centuries turned into millennia, there was too much work to leave any time for reflection on their past, and indeed it was just forgotten until one day, some 80 000 years later, the descendants of Sarah's people became aware.

Over a mere few hundred years they reinvented the science and technology that had been long forgotten, the legend was rediscovered in an ancient manuscript, and they turned their telescopes toward the bright star in the Southern sky around which, they were sure, circled the "Planet of the Double Sun".

We developed space travel.

We're going Home!

Afterword:

So we are the descendants of Sarah's people. If you look towards the South in the evening sky you will see a yellow star – one of the "pointers" below the Southern Cross. This is Alpha Centauri A, which is indeed our sun's twin, and yes, it does have a companion, Alpha Centauri B which, seen from a planet as far from Alpha Centauri A as our Earth is from the sun, would appear about 150 times as bright as the full moon, so there is no doubt that it would be something rather special to any inhabitants of that planet.

The journey time of 800 years is perfectly realistic, in terms of energy requirements, and the concept of "Generation Ships" is certainly not new. Neither is the idea of using hollowed-out asteroids to save building a spacecraft from scratch. Such a craft would hold sufficient atmosphere to have genuine weather systems, and the spin along the long axis would indeed give the effect of artificial gravity.

The plot to some extent complements the currently popular "Out of Africa" theory of evolution, except, of course, the theory suggests that the human species evolved naturally, rather than arriving from elsewhere so…

…it's just a story.

But how do you explain the legend?